SIMPLY APPLIQUE

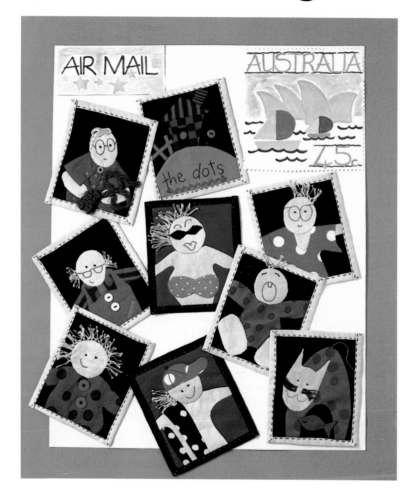

Yolanda Gifford

A J.B. Fairfax Press Publication

EDITORIAL
MANAGING EDITOR
Judy Poulos

EDITORIAL ASSISTANT
Ella Martin

EDITORIAL COORDINATOR
Margaret Kelly

PHOTOGRAPHY
Richard Weinstein

STYLING
Kathy Tripp

ILLUSTRATION
Lesley Griffith

PRODUCTION AND DESIGN
PRODUCTION DIRECTOR
Anna Maguire

LAYOUT
Lulu Dougherty

DESIGN MANAGER
Drew Buckmaster

PRODUCTION CO-ORDINATOR
Sophie Potter

CONCEPT DESIGN
Jenny Pace

PUBLISHED BY J.B. FAIRFAX PRESS PTY LIMITED
80-82 MCLACHLAN AVE
RUSHCUTTERS BAY
AUSTRALIA 2011
A.C.N. 003 738 430

FORMATTED BY J.B. FAIRFAX PRESS PTY LIMITED

PRINTED BY TOPPAN PRINTING CO. SINGAPORE
© J.B. FAIRFAX PRESS PTY LIMITED 1997

JBFP 477

SIMPLY APPLIQUE
ISBN 1 86343 303 1

DISTRIBUTION AND SALES
Tel: (02) 9361 6366 Fax: (02) 9360 6262
http://www.jbfp.com.au

Contents

About the Author	4
Simply Appliqué Basics	6
THE PROJECTS	10
Quilt of Scraps	12
Christmas Tablecloth	15
Family Portrait	18
Kitchen Curtains	23
Sunset	30
Two Appliquéd Cushions	34
The Three Sisters	38
Dot Family Postcards	42
Bright Wall Quilt	47
Japanese Bag	54
Embroidered Cot Quilt	58
The Love Quilt	65
Star Tablecloth	68
Animal Banner	72
The Spotted Heart	76
Acknowledgments	80

About the Author

My love of colour and fabric has been with me since early childhood when I watched my grandmother patching dolls on her bed. This led me to start making dolls and 'patchy things'.

After leaving school I graduated in fashion and design and ended up working in South Africa. I finally returned to Sydney, Australia, dragging all my fabrics and patterns around the world with me.

Settled down with a family, I explored my love of fabric once again — this time in patchwork; twelve years later, I feel I'm just beginning!

I started teaching young children sewing craft and this led to my first book Fabric Fun For Kids. I still teach children, and have found in their wonderful sense of colour and freedom of style, a new outlet for teaching adults a simple naive style of appliqué. My methods are non-traditional and are based on freedom in colour, design and structure. My quilts just happen and are not worked to any specific size or measurement. Instead of using scissors, I like to rip or tear fabric to a suitable size, and I have never used a rotary cutter!

A quilt must be a visual delight and is finished when I reach that end result. Quilts are about families and friends and stories we love to cherish, and they should be an abundance of colour and expression.

Wrap yourself in the colour and warmth of your very own quilt as you work through these pages and, most importantly, let yourself go!

Simply Appliqué Basics

Please read all these directions thoroughly before starting your project.

MATERIALS

Embroidery threads

Stranded cotton comes in skeins of six strands and is usually separated into lengths of two strands. Separate the strands by pulling them apart very gently or the threads will knot. Silk embroidery thread does not separate easily and is best used as is.

Embroidery embellishments

For embroidery to be a feature on your quilt, you must use six strands of embroidery thread. Large, bold and simple stitches make an interesting effect. If the stitches are to be fine and detailed, one strand of thread is sufficient. Sometimes, using both methods together can be very effective.

Fabric

All fabric should be washed in warm, soapy water, then rinsed and pressed before you start to sew. Bright and dark colours may need a handful of salt in the water to stop them from bleeding. In this book, I have used many different fabrics – for example, flannels, velvets, lurex and cottons – and have washed them all. Take care pressing fabrics such as lurex.

Needles

Needles are a personal matter – a bit like choosing a face cream – but, if it helps, I use a size 9 straw needle for needleturning appliqué. For traditional appliqué, I use a size 10 appliqué needle. A size 7 crewel needle is great for sewing with embroidery thread.

Templates

A medium-density cardboard is very good for making templates of pattern pieces. Using a pencil, trace the pattern from the book, cut it out, then trace around it on the cardboard. Cut it out very carefully on the pencil line. Cardboard templates can then be discarded when they are no longer required.

Wadding

This can vary according to the effect you want to achieve. A thin wadding makes quilting easy work; cotton is harder to sew, but looks lovely after washing, and wool is thick and warm. Choose one to suit your needs and follow the manufacturer's instructions for use and care.

SKILLS

Pressing

When ironing pieced blocks together, always press the seams to one side, preferably towards the darker fabric. When pressing Vliesofix onto fabric, never move the iron back and forth. Always press down hard and hold it for a few seconds. Do this two or three times. Make sure the Vliesofix is exactly the same size as the fabric or you will have a messy iron afterwards!

Quilting

For quilting, mark the desired pattern onto the front of the fabric with a soft lead or yellow pencil. For quilting around appliqué, use a traditional quilting thread. If you wish to make your quilting a feature, use two strands of an embroidery thread. 'Quilt of Scraps' on page 12 was stitched in this way.

Seam allowances

All seam allowances in the book are to be 1 cm (3/8 in) unless stated otherwise. For needleturning appliqué, the seam allowance should be 5 mm (1/4 in). The smaller the seam allowance, the easier it is to turn it under with the needle.

Tea-dyeing

Tea-dyeing is great for giving modern fabrics a soft, aged appearance. Fill a large saucepan with water and add six tea bags – the more tea you use, the darker the fabric will be. Bring the water to the boil, place the wet fabric into the pot and stir. Take the pot off the heat and allow it to sit for thirty minutes. Rinse the fabric under cold water.

Tying buttons

Buttons are a wonderful feature on quilts. They can be sewn on or tied on, using up to six strands of embroidery thread. Starting at the front of your work, go through the buttonholes twice, then tie two knots on the front. Cut the thread to the desired length, but no less than 1 cm (3/8 in).

Tying a quilt

A quilt can be tied instead of quilted. Mark evenly spaced points on your quilt. Using six strands of embroidery thread, push the needle through from the top of the work to the back and up to the top again, just 6 mm (1/4 in) away. Tie a double knot firmly and cut the thread approximately 1 cm (3/8 in) away. Buttons can be used in combination with this type of quilting.

METHODS OF APPLIQUE

Needleturning appliqué

Trace the pattern onto the front of the fabric with a soft pencil, then cut it out, approximately 5 mm (^{1}/4 in) outside the pencil line. Cut into any corners or curves to allow the fabric to turn under neatly. Place the appliqué piece on the background and either pin or baste it into position. Using a size 9 sewing needle, turn under the seam allowance, folding back the fabric up to the pencil line. Sew the appliqué with an invisible slipstitch. Match the thread to the appliqué, NOT to the background fabric. It is easiest if you turn the fabric a little, sew it, then turn the next little bit of fabric. Do not try to do too much at once.

Traditional appliqué

Trace the pattern as before and transfer it to cardboard. Cut out the cardboard on the pencil line. Using the cardboard template, draw the pattern onto the back of the fabric. Cut it out with a 1 cm (^{3}/8 in) seam allowance all around. Clip into any curves (Fig. 1). Baste the fabric piece tightly around the cardboard, right side out. (Fig. 2). Press with a hot iron until it is completely flat. Remove the cardboard and baste the appliqué piece into position on the background. Slipstitch it into place using a matching thread (Fig. 3).

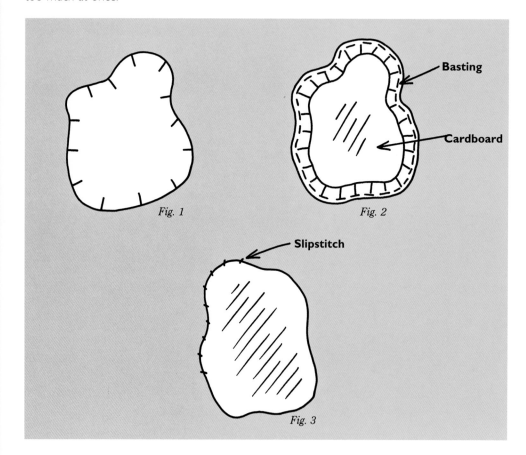

Fig. 1

Fig. 2

Basting

Cardboard

Slipstitch

Fig. 3

Vliesofix appliqué

Trace the pattern as before and transfer it to cardboard. Cut out the cardboard on the pencil line. Trace the pattern onto the right side of the fabric, using the cardboard template. Do not cut out the shape, but cut out a square around it (Fig. 4). Cut a similar-sized piece of Vliesofix and place the sticky side to the back of the fabric. Press the two pieces together with a very hot iron. Cut out the pattern exactly on the pencil line. Peel the backing off the Vliesofix and position it, sticky side down, in the place where it is to be appliquéd. Press with a hot iron as before. It is not recommended that you lift Vliesofix once it is ironed, so take care to position it correctly the first time!

Using one or two strands of embroidery thread, sew a very small chain stitch around the outside edge of the Vliesofix. This will give the Vliesofix a slightly raised look. It is important that you stitch on the edge of the pattern piece and not beside it (Fig. 5).

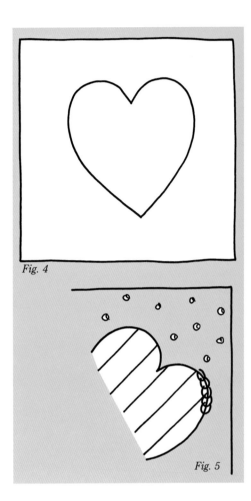

Fig. 4

Fig. 5

The Projects

The images and designs in this book are all about colour and fun. They are simple and carefree and flow along with a childlike quality that is not difficult to follow. The whole essence is to be free in your stitching and use of colour and to allow your imagination to move along the fabric and flow into your work!

Try using children's drawings for inspiration and never throw any of their artwork away. When caught out for ideas, it's fabulous to sift through their work and absorb as much as possible of their simple style.

The use of plain fabrics helps to make the image stronger and appears to give a more definite outline. Lots of plain colours together make a very strong statement. When the plains are used on a white background, they soften and appear pure, clear and crisp.

Life is full of colour and, by surrounding ourselves with colour, we feel its energy and strength.

Flowers and planter from Pigott's Store, Woollahra NSW

Quilt of Scraps

- as many different-coloured scraps of fabric as you can find
- approximately 2 m (2¹/4 yd) of fabric for the border
- approximately 4 m (4¹/2 yd) of fabric for the backing
- approximately 4 m (4¹/2 yd) of cotton wadding
- rickrack braid, yo yo flowers, buttons, sequins and other embellishments
- embroidery threads
- usual sewing supplies

Note: This quilt does not have exact material measurements because it depends on what fabric you have available and what you want to use. I tried to keep each fabric different, using all my favourites as well as my leftovers, and just ripped and sewed until I reached the size that seemed right.

Once you get the hang of it, making a scrap quilt like this is so easy because you don't need a pattern, there are no rules and it can grow in whatever direction you choose.

Finished size: 195 cm × 205 cm (79 in × 83 in)

I started with a purple dot fabric which measured 14 cm × 20 cm (5¹/2 in × 8 in). I then added a scrap of red to one end. The yellow floral strip came after that and then the stripe. To this I added the large striped piece on the right, then the star fabric above. I had some pieces already sewn together – leftover from a previous quilt – so in they went. (I liken it to making a risotto where you can throw in any leftovers you have at hand, and the more flavours you add the better it tastes.) For my fabric layout in the centre piece and as a guide to get you going, see figure 1.

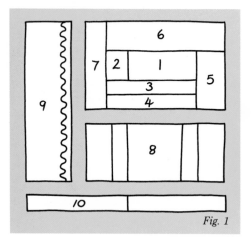

Fig. 1

The finished size of the centre piece is 134 cm × 140 cm (51¹/2 in × 55 in) and that's because I ran out of scraps! The blue borders are 34 cm (13¹/2 in) wide. When I found I didn't have enough fabric, in went the blue-and-black check.

To add a bit of interest, make a panel of appliqué hearts and mini Log Cabin blocks and small squares. Using smaller blocks together with larger makes it more interesting, and adding a bit of appliqué here and there is also fun.

The possibilities for this type of quilt are endless – think what a wonderful picnic rug you could make. The beauty is also in the choice of fabrics. This quilt has velvet, flannel, lurex, Japanese prints and cotton fabrics.

When making a dramatic quilt, I love a strong finish on the back, but if you use light fabrics, a lovely pastel floral would be gorgeous. Gingham on the back for a child would be practical and fun.

For the wadding, I chose cotton, but any wadding could be used.

When I came to quilt, I wasn't sure what to do on such a scrappy top, so overlapping stars seemed to be the answer. Once I started, I couldn't stop and so many hours of quilting have added to the overall texture and effect. A bright zany border to finish, made a nice touch.

After making this quilt, I know I'll be making more just like it. I haven't had so much fun making a quilt in a long time.

Quilt of Scraps

Christmas Tablecloth

This tablecloth can also be made out of different fabric scraps and used all year round as a picnic rug. It's a very quick and easy quilt to sew, and anyone who has problems with their hands will find the method of tearing instead of cutting with scissors much easier to manage.

Finished size: 106 cm × 204 cm (41 1/2 in × 82 1/2 in)

INSTRUCTIONS
See the pattern on page 16.

Preparation
Cut or tear the Christmas fabrics into 15 cm (6 in) wide strips and any length from 6 cm (2 3/8 in) to 36 cm (14 in). Try to have a large variety of lengths in as many different fabrics as possible. Place them all in a basket and mix them up so no two fabrics the same are together.

Assembling
1   Choose any two fabrics and sew the 15 cm (6 in) sides together. Then choose another fabric from the basket and stitch this on to the first two. Keep going in this way until you reach a length of 2 m (2 1/4 yd). You may wish to adjust this length to suit yourself. Make ten of these lengths. Arrange them in rows, then join them together lengthwise. Occasionally, fabrics will overlap, but this adds to the lovely random flavour of the quilt. Trim the seams.

2   Cut 25 cm (10 in) wide border strips that are 2 m (2 1/4 yd) long. Sew a border to each side of the top piece. Trim the ends, then sew the top and bottom borders into place.

3   For the back, sew all the leftover scraps together to make a border around the red gingham. This border can vary in width – about 20 cm (8 in) is a good size. Stitch the border pieces to the top and bottom and both sides of the gingham, then adjust the backing to suit the size of your top. More scraps can be added around the edge or you can adjust the size of the top border. Press both pieces well.

4   Place the top piece, right side down, and position the back piece on top, right side up. Carefully fold over the front border onto the back, pin it down and turn under a small hem. The back may have to be trimmed to suit. Fold in the

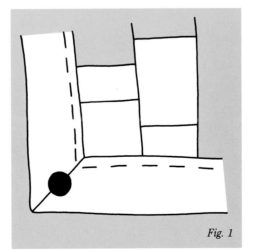

Fig. 1

corners envelope-style. Using two strands of Red embroidery thread, sew around the hem in a running stitch. The stitches should show through to the front, so keep them as even as possible. On the right side, sew a red button in each corner (Fig. 1).

Appliqué

1 Trace the pattern and transfer it to the cardboard. Cut out the star and use it for the template.

2 Cut out a total of fourteen 18 cm (7 in) squares from the red and yellow fabrics. Using the cardboard template, cut out fourteen red and yellow stars. Pin a red star in the centre of the yellow squares and a yellow star into the centre of the red squares. Stitch around the stars in Green thread, approximately 1 cm ($3/8$ in) from the edge.

3 Appliqué the star patches all over the tablecloth, using two strands of either Red or Yellow thread, depending on the colour of the patch, and stitching approximately 1 cm ($3/8$ in) from the edge. This stitching will go through to the back of the tablecloth, and it can be repeated as a quilting pattern, even where there are no patches. When the patches are sewn, fray the edges a little as shown.

4 Cut out extra red and yellow stars and appliqué these in between the star patches. I have added seven stars, but you can add as many as you like, or even appliqué an entire border of stars around the tablecloth, if you wish.

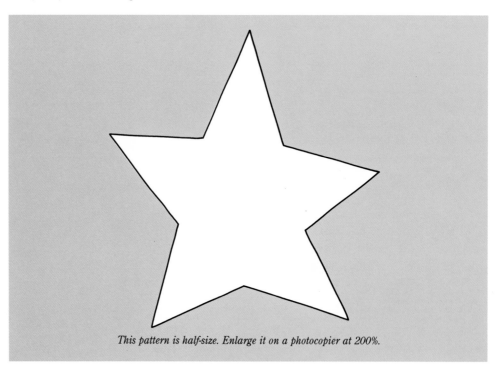

This pattern is half-size. Enlarge it on a photocopier at 200%.

Family Portrait

YOU WILL NEED

- 36 cm x 44 cm (14 in x 18 in) of background fabric
- 25 cm (10 in) of homespun
- small scraps of old family clothing
- scraps of felt
- 50 cm (20 in) of fabric for the border
- 40 cm x 50 cm (16 in x 20 in) of Pellon
- 40 cm x 50 cm (16 in x 20 in) of homespun for the backing
- embellishments: hair, braid, buttons, embroidery threads, jewellery etc
- picture frame, 40 cm x 50 cm (16 in x 20 in)
- masking tape
- cardboard for the templates
- medium-weight cardboard, 40 cm x 50 cm (16 in x 20 in) for the backing
- matching sewing threads
- stranded embroidery cotton for the features and hair
- tracing paper
- pencil

For the background, I used our old kitchen curtains; the faded brown makes an interesting backdrop. An old bedspread or sheet, or checked tea towel would also be suitable.

Finished size: 40 cm x 50 cm (16 in x 20 in)

INSTRUCTIONS
See the patterns on pages 21–22.

Preparation
1 Trace the people from the pattern, adjusting the number, size and sex of family members to suit your own family. Once you have the appropriate patterns drawn, transfer them to the cardboard, then cut them out to use as templates.
2 Tea-dye the piece of homespun.
3 Using the fabrics from the old clothing of family members, draw around the patterns on the right side of the fabrics. Cut out the fabric pieces slightly larger than the pencil outline. Cut out all the faces, hands and legs from the homespun. As each figure is cut out, it's a good idea to store it in a labelled envelope, as there are a lot of little bits for each person. When the family is cut out, any animals can be added.

Appliqué
1 Position the cut-out pieces on the background, using the picture as a guide, and overlapping them where necessary. Baste the figures down first, as this makes sewing them onto the background a lot easier. Starting with the larger figures at the back and using a matching thread, needleturn around the edges of each piece. When all the main figures are sewn on, add the animals.

2 For the embellishments, sew on pockets, names on shirts, buttons, hearts, earrings, toys, bells on animals and dog leads (I used a piece of wool). The faces are embroidered in back stitch with French knots for the eyes. The shoes are felt. For straight hair, use stranded cotton, catching about twelve pieces in the centre of the head. For curly hair, use a good doll's hair. A moustache or beard can also be added now. If you have a special fabric, add this around the family or embroider your surname.

Assembling

1 When the portrait is completed, place it right side up on top of the Pellon and the backing fabric. Baste the three layers together and quilt around each family member.

2 Cut two border strips, 10 cm x 36 cm (4 in x 14 in). Machine-stitch the borders to the top and bottom, through all three layers. Cut two more strips, each 10 cm x 56 cm (4 in x 22 in) and stitch them to either side.

This pattern is half-size. Enlarge it on a photocopier at 200%.

TO FINISH

Place the portrait right side up on the piece of medium-weight cardboard and tape the fabric onto the back by pulling it over the cardboard tightly and taping it securely on all four sides. Place the picture into the frame and lock it into position. You will have to remove the glass from the frame as all the embellishments will make the picture too thick. Without glass, the portrait will collect dust over time, but a light vacuum or shake is all that is necessary to keep it clean. Make sure you protect the portrait from strong sunlight or you will all fade away!

Kitchen Curtains

This style of curtain looks great with large wooden rings showing at the top edge, and the nice thing about these curtains is that no two curtains will be exactly the same.

INSTRUCTIONS
See a selection of suitable patterns on pages 24 and 26–29.

Preparation
1 Cut the curtain fabric in half so you have two lengths – one for each side of the window. The finished size of the curtains must be the same as the window, so the appliqué is clearly visible and not hidden in folds of fabric.
2 If you are using scraps for the bottom border, cut them into random lengths that are all 8 cm (3¼ in) wide. Join them together to make a long strip that is the same length as the curtain width. Sew the pieced border to the bottom edge of the curtain.
3 Sew the 6 cm (2½ in) wide strips to the sides of the curtain.
4 Measure the length of the window and adjust the length of the curtain (from the top) to suit the window, curtain pole and fittings. Sew the 20 cm (8 in) wide

strip to the top of each curtain. Fold it in half with the wrong sides together, turn under the raw edge and stitch it to the main curtain fabric. The finished top piece will now be 10 cm (4 in) wide.

Appliqué
1 Trace the appliqué patterns and transfer them onto the cardboard. Cut them out for templates. Trace around the templates on the right side of the tea-dyed scraps. Cut them out, leaving a 5 mm (¼ in) seam allowance around each piece.
2 Arrange the motifs in a pleasing design, then pin them to the bottom edge of the main curtain fabric, not on the border. Using the needleturn method and matching thread, appliqué each motif into place. Press well.
3 The chimneys, doors and windows are not hemmed, but are appliquéd with the raw edges showing. You could hem them, if you prefer. Embellish the doors on the houses and the eyes on the people and animals with buttons. If you want to make a feature of the stitching, use two strands of an embroidery thread and bold stitches for applying the appliqué.

TO FINISH
1 Hem the sides and bottom edge of the curtains with a small running stitch. Cut the backing fabric to the same size as the curtains and hem the sides and bottom.
2 Mark a line on the inside edge, 1 cm (3/8 in) down from the top of the striped border. Machine-stitch a length of curtain tape straight across. Slip the backing fabric under the lower edge of the curtain tape, then stitch across, joining all three layers together. Pull up the tape cords to suit your window. Attach the rings and hang the curtains.

YOU WILL NEED
- piece of curtain fabric the same size as the inside measurements of your window
- piece of fabric 20 cm (8 in) wide and the same width as the curtains for the top
- four pieces of fabric, each one 6 cm (2½ in) wide by the length of the curtain
- piece of fabric, 8 cm (3¼ in) wide and the same width as the curtain for the bottom edge (I have used scraps)
- scraps of fabric for the appliqué
- length of curtain tape
- wooden curtain rings
- heavy fabric for the backing
- embroidery thread
- buttons and other embellishments
- usual sewing supplies
- cardboard
- ordinary sewing threads to match the fabrics
- tracing paper
- pencil

Note: Before starting, I tea-dyed an assortment of fabrics and all the curtain lengths to give them an old country look. Using a heavy backing fabric will protect your appliquéd curtains so they will last for years.

Sunset

This little wallhanging is very simple. If you use the Vliesofix method of appliqué, it can be finished very quickly. The chain stitching over the edge of the appliqué adds a nice finishing touch. This would be a very good practice piece, before working on the Appliqué Cushions on page 34.

Finished size: 32 cm x 56 cm (12¹/₂ in x 22 in)

INSTRUCTIONS

See the patterns on pages 32–33.

Appliqué

1 Trace the patterns and transfer them to the cardboard. Cut them out to use as templates.
2 Apply Vliesofix to the back of the scraps for the appliqué. Place the cardboard patterns onto the Vliesofix and trace around them. Cut out carefully along the pencil line.

3 Remove the backing from the Vliesofix and iron the pieces into position on the main fabric, using the picture as a guide. Note that the flowers will overlap the stems.
4 Using two strands of a matching embroidery thread and a tiny chain stitch, sew around the edges of the appliqué pieces. For the bird's eye, sew a French knot.

Assembling

1 Lay the backing fabric, right side down and centre the wadding on the top. Centre the appliquéd top on the wadding, facing up. Bring the backing fabric over onto the front and turn under a small hem, leaving a 2 cm (³/₄ in) border showing on the front. Using two strands of embroidery thread and running stitches, sew around the edge, keeping the stitches even.
2 Using one strand of embroidery thread, quilt in a small stitch around all the appliqué shapes, just outside the chain stitch. Do this as many times as you like.

TO FINISH

Cut three pieces of fabric, each 5 cm x 14 cm (2 in x 5¹/₂ in). Fold them over and sew to form tubes. Turn them to the right side. Stitch the open ends together to the back of the quilt, so that 4 cm (1¹/₂ in) is showing above the top edge. Insert a rod and hang your little quilt for all to admire.

Two Appliquéd Cushions

What a lovely way to relax – on a pile of beautiful soft cushions. These would be equally at home on a cane chair, a lounge or a bed with white linen. Using the Vliesofix method of appliqué and the added chain-stitch embroidery, makes it simple to achieve the perfect cushion with no buttonholes or zippers.

Finished size: 46 cm (18 in) square

INSTRUCTIONS
See the patterns on pages 36–37.

Preparation
1 Trace the appliqué patterns, then transfer them onto cardboard. Cut them out to use as templates.
2 Place the templates onto the cotton scraps, using the picture on page 35 as a guide, and draw around them. Do not cut out the shape, but cut out a square around each traced pattern. Cut the same-sized square out of Vliesofix.
3 Iron the Vliesofix onto the back of the fabric squares, then cut out the pattern shape exactly.

Appliqué
1 Position the shapes on the smaller white homespun square as shown in the picture. Remove the backing from the Vliesofix and press the pieces into place.
2 Using two strands of a matching embroidery thread and a very small chain stitch, sew around each shape, right on the edge.
   Note: When appliquéing pieces, make sure the embroidery thread is well

secured at the back and the threads cut short. Because this design uses strong colours on white homespun, any threads that hang will show through to the front if they are not cut and tucked well under.
3 Sew the bird's legs in back stitch, using one strand of thread. The eyes are French knots.

Assembling
1 Sew a yellow-checked strip to two sides of the centre square, then stitch a yellow square to each end of the two remaining yellow strips (Fig. 1). Stitch these two strips to the other two sides.
2 Lay the top piece, right side up, over the two 46 cm (18 in) homespun squares, then trim all three layers to the same size with pinking shears.
3 Pin the three layers together and, keeping them very flat, tie a button in each of the four corners, using six strands of the Yellow embroidery

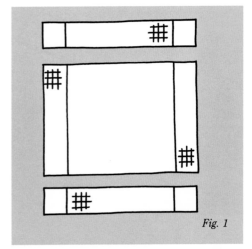

Fig. 1

thread. Tie five buttons, equally spaced, on each yellow-check border. When three sides of the cushion are completed, pop the insert between the two white homespun squares. The cushion insert should not fit firmly, but rather be a little small so that the edge sits loosely around the cushion. This gives a much softer appearance.

The Three Sisters

Cot from Flash Trash, Camperdown NSW

YOU WILL NEED

- ■ 10 cm (4 in) of tea-dyed homespun
- ■ scraps of brightly coloured spotted and checked fabrics
- ■ 10 cm (4 in) of black homespun
- ■ natural sheep's wool for the hair
- ■ sewing threads to match the hair
- ■ brightly coloured dyes for the hair
- ■ embroidery threads
- ■ small amount of doll's stuffing
- ■ braid, buttons, lace
- ■ tracing paper
- ■ pencil
- ■ cardboard
- ■ string
- ■ black permanent marker pen

A funny trio, these little dolls are not difficult to sew. They dangle very sweetly under a sign, or dance over the fireplace. The dolls can be made individually, or you can make as many as you like. You can wear them, hang them or dangle them. If you have a sister, you could make one to look like her!

Finished size: 16 cm (6¼ in) tall

INSTRUCTIONS

See the patterns on page 41.

Preparation

1 Trace the patterns and transfer them to the cardboard. Cut them out to use as templates. Cut out the cardboard templates.

2 Place all the templates onto the wrong side of the selected fabrics and trace around them. The main body pieces will be homespun, with the brightly coloured fabric for the legs and the black homespun for the shoes. The black fabric is stitched to the leg fabric, before tracing the pattern, so that the shoe and leg are traced as one piece (Fig. 1).

Assembling

1 Stitch the main body first, leaving the bottom end open. Turn it right side out and stuff it firmly. Close the bottom end. Sew both legs and shoes, leaving the top open. Turn the legs right side out and stuff them firmly. Stitch the top of the legs onto the base of the body.

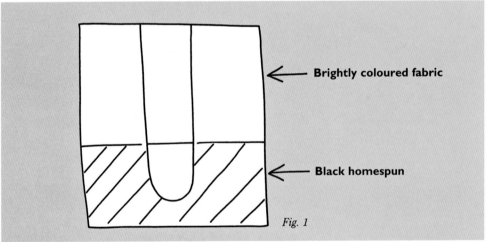

Brightly coloured fabric

Black homespun

Fig. 1

2   Add the embellishments to the dresses before sewing. Stitch the sides of the dress, turn them right side out and pop them on the dolls. Using four strands of embroidery thread and starting at the front of the dress, sew a running stitch around the neck edge. Draw up the thread tightly and tie a double knot. Repeat the same procedure for the sleeves.

3   Dye the sheep's wool in the colours of your choice. Stitch the hair around the head in a small running stitch, using matching thread.

4   Embroider the eyes and mouth, and draw on the nose, eyebrows, freckles etc with the marker pen.

5   Join the dolls together at their hands as shown. Attach a length of string to the outside hands and tie a loop ready for hanging. The dolls are also a perfect size to wear as a brooch – all you need is a safety pin stitched onto the back.

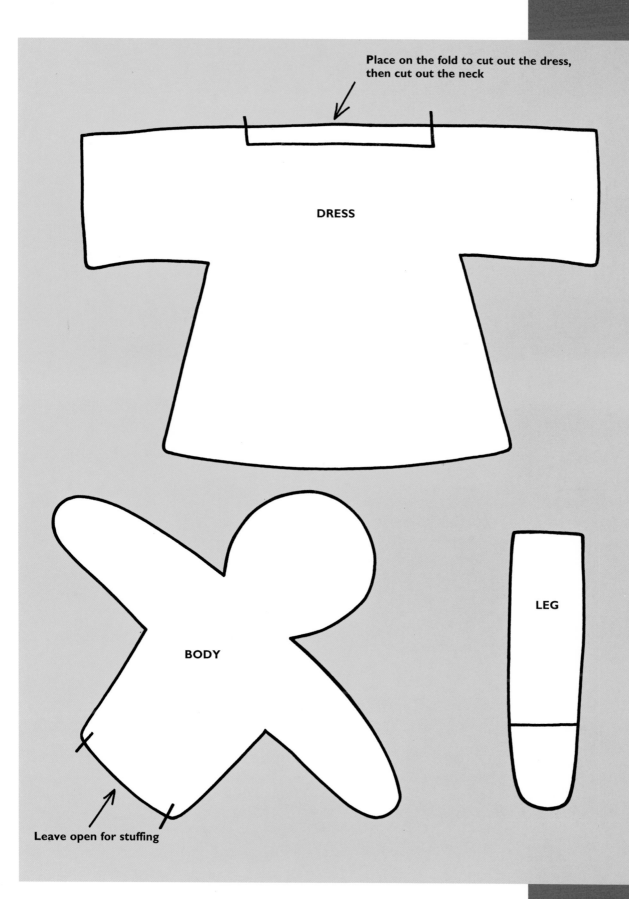

Place on the fold to cut out the dress, then cut out the neck

DRESS

BODY

LEG

Leave open for stuffing

Dot Family
Postcards

This little comic family is a fun project and the family could be extended to include an aunt, uncle, dog or even the family car! Each piece should come to life with a character of its own. Another idea could be to stitch your very own fabric portraits of the ones you love and hang them on the wall.

Finished size: 15 cm x 18 cm (6 in x 7 in)

INSTRUCTIONS
See the patterns on pages 44–46.

Preparation
1 Trace the patterns and transfer them onto cardboard. Label each part. Cut them out to use as templates.
2 Place the patterns onto the front of the chosen fabrics and draw around the shapes in pencil, leaving a 5 mm (¹/₄ in) seam allowance on each piece. Cut out each piece with the seam allowance.

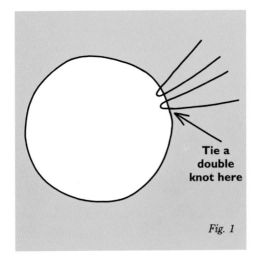

Tie a double knot here

Fig. 1

Appliqué
1 Using the needleturn method and matching thread, appliqué the pieces onto the background fabric. Start with the largest back pieces, then overlap them with the smaller front pieces. The head is always appliquéd last of all. These pictures can also be sewn on using a fabric adhesive or the traditional method of appliqué over paper or card.
2 When all the main pictures are sewn on, stitch in the details. For the mouths, use three strands of embroidery thread and back stitch. All the other details are sewn with one strand of thread. Attach buttons where shown. Stitch the hair as shown in figure 1. For Grandma's knitting, knit a little square, leaving 20 cm (8 in) free on the end of the wool. Sew the piece of knitting onto Grandma's hands with slipstitches and embroider on

AIR MAIL

AUSTRALIA

the dots

45c

the needles. Grandma's hair was wrapped in a loop and stitched down on either side, then running stitches were used on the side of her head.

Assembling

When all the pictures are completed, place them face down on the table, with the Pellon on top, then the backing fabric, right side up. Turn the layers over. The backing is larger all around than the other two layers, enabling you to turn under a small hem onto the right side of the picture. There should be approximately 1 cm (3/8 in) of the backing showing on the front. Sew around the edges with running stitches, using two strands of embroidery thread.

These patterns are half-size. Enlarge them on a photocopier at 200%.

These patterns are half-size. Enlarge them on a photocopier at 200%.

These patterns are half-size. Enlarge them on a photocopier at 200%.

Bright Wall Quilt

A happy and bright little quilt, this could hang in the hall or on a child's wall. It would be delightful made into a single bed quilt or tucked into a cot. Simple to make using the traditional method of appliqué, this is a good project for beginners.

Finished size: 90 cm x 110 cm (36 in x 44 in)

INSTRUCTIONS

See the patterns on pages 48 and 50–53

Appliqué

1 You will need to make nine blocks, each one 20 cm x 30 cm (8 in x 12 in) plus seam allowances, out of the assorted fabrics. Start by choosing a main colour, cut to any size, then add a bottom and a top fabric, making sure each block is different from the next. If the fabric is too narrow to use, then just add a strip down the side to make up the difference. The fun part in making these blocks is that any fabric will do, and if it's not big enough, then you just add a little here and a little there! Make nine wonderfully colourful blocks.

2 Trace the appliqué patterns, then transfer them onto the cardboard and cut them out for templates. Trace around each template onto the fabric scraps, using the picture as a guide. Cut them out, leaving a small seam allowance all around. Appliqué a pattern onto the main centre fabric of each block. You can use any method of appliqué for these blocks, matching the thread to the fabric that is appliquéd. For the bird design, back stitch the legs, wing and eyes. Stitch the seeds in French knots.

Assembling

1 Cut six strips, each 7 cm x 30 cm (3 in x 12 in) plus seam allowances from six different fabrics. Sew one to the side of each block so when they are laid out, you have one block, one strip, one block, one strip, one block (Fig. 1). Make three rows. Join the rows with a 6 cm x 76 cm (2¹/₂ in x 30¹/₂ in) strip in between them. You will need four of these strips, including strips for the top and the bottom (Fig. 2).

2 Trim the edges of the quilt so they are even and straight. Sew the two

YOU WILL NEED

- 25 cm (10 in) scraps of twenty different bright fabrics
- two pieces of blue fabric, each 7 cm x 109 cm (3 in x 43 in)
- four pieces of four different bright fabrics, each 6 cm x 77 m (2¹/₂ in x 30¹/₂ in)
- 1 m (1¹/₈ yd) of checked fabric for the binding
- 90 cm x 110 cm (36 in x 44 in) of wadding
- 90 cm x 110 cm (36 in x 44 in) of fabric for the backing
- small amounts of embroidery thread
- usual sewing supplies
- cardboard
- tracing paper
- pencil

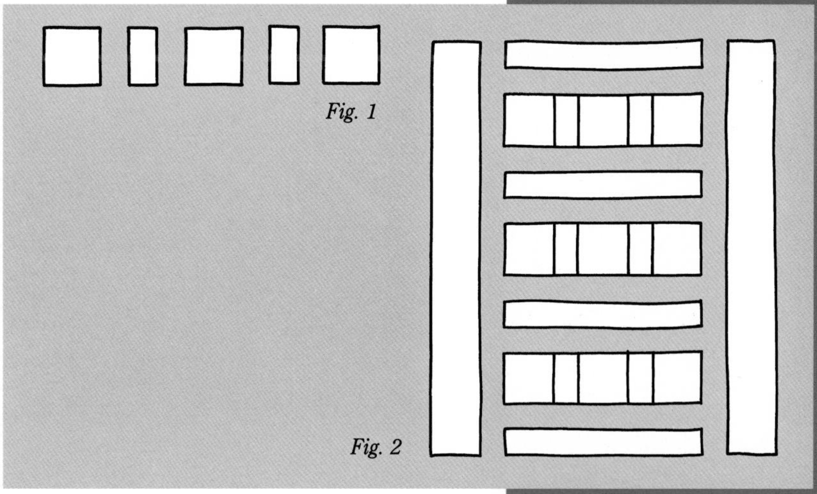

Fig. 1

Fig. 2

remaining pieces of blue fabric down the sides of the quilt. Neaten the edges.

TO FINISH

1   Cut the binding fabric into 6 cm (2¹/₂ in) wide strips. Attach them to the top and bottom of the quilt front, with the right sides together, then to the sides. Press open.

2   Place the quilt face down; position the wadding in the centre, then the backing fabric on top, with the right side facing you. Trim the wadding and the backing fabric to the size of the top piece. Baste all three layers together.

3   Turn the binding over to the back, leaving approximately 2 cm (³/₄ in) showing on the right side. Turn under the raw edge. With a small slipstitch and matching thread, sew the binding on the back.

4   Quilt around each of the blocks as desired.

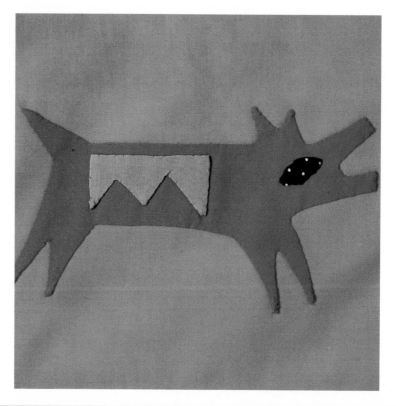

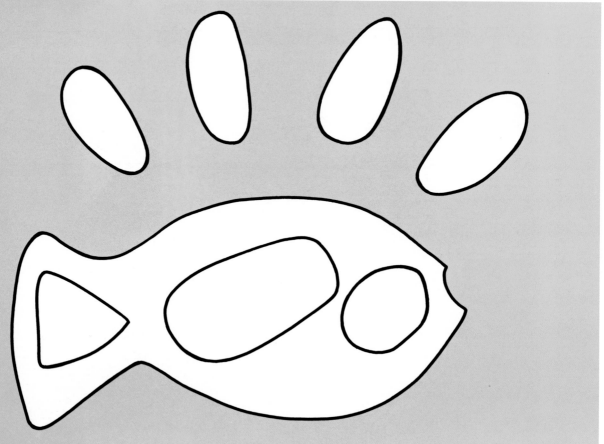

Japanese Bag

YOU WILL NEED

- **28 cm x 45 cm (11 in x 18 in) of main fabric for the bag**
- **20 cm (8 in) square of fabric for the base**
- **20 cm (8 in) square of firm wadding**
- **30 cm x 65 cm (12 in x 25¹/2 in) of fabric for the lining**
- **14 cm x 18 cm (5¹/2 in x 7 in) of homespun for the front**
- **assorted scraps of fabric for appliqué**
- **75 cm (29¹/2 in) of cord**
- **eight small rings**
- **four buttons**
- **embroidery threads**
- **small amount of Vliesofix**
- **sewing thread to match the fabrics**
- **usual sewing supplies**
- **tracing paper**
- **cardboard**
- **pencil**

Fig. 1

This little 'handy bag' made up from Japanese fabrics can be lined for a toiletry bag or used to hold all the little bits and pieces that we all accumulate. Made up in a glamorous fabric, the same bag would be a lovely evening accessory.

INSTRUCTIONS

See the patterns on pages 56–57.

Appliqué

1. Trace the tree pattern, then transfer it onto the cardboard. Cut out the shapes.
2. Iron Vliesofix onto the wrong side of the selected tree fabrics.
3. Place the cardboard patterns onto the right side of the fabrics and draw around them in pencil. Cut out exactly on the pencil line.
4. Position the trees on the piece of homespun. Peel off the Vliesofix and press the trees with a hot iron until the pieces are firmly adhered to the background.
5. Sew a running stitch around the inside edge of the appliqué with two strands of embroidery thread.

Assembling

1. Fold the main bag fabric in half so it measures 22.5 cm x 28 cm (9 in x 11 in). Position the appliquéd homespun in the centre of one half, leaving room at the top for turning the cord casing. Stitch the homespun into place using one strand of embroidery thread and a small running stitch. Sew a button in each corner (Fig. 1). Leave the edges raw and fray them a little. If you wish to turn under the raw edge, you will need to add a seam allowance when cutting out the homespun.

2. With the right sides together, stitch the side seam of the bag.
3. Using a matching thread, sew running stitches around the base of the bag, pulling the thread gently to slightly gather the edge.
4. Cut out the base oval from the base fabric. Turn the bag inside out. Place the right sides of the bag and the oval together and gently ease them, adjusting the gathering stitch, if necessary, to form a nice even curve. Stitch the two together just under the gathering stitch. Turn right side out.
5. From the lining fabric, cut one piece 28 cm x 45 cm (11 in x 18 in) and one oval base. Stitch the short sides of the rectangle together and ease the oval base onto the bag lining in exactly the same way as for the main bag.
6. Cut an oval base from the wadding and place it in the bottom of the main bag, then push the lining down gently so the two wrong sides are facing and the side seams line up.
7. Turn down a 1 cm (³/8 in) hem at the top of the main bag and turn down the lining towards the main bag, allowing the lining to extend by 5 mm (¹/4 in). Running stitch the bag and the lining together around the top edge, using two strands of embroidery thread.

TO FINISH

1. Place the small rings, equally spaced around the bag, 2.5 cm (1 in) from the top. Stitch the rings into place using a matching thread.
2. Starting from the centre front of the bag, thread the cord through all the rings and tie the ends together in a knot.

BASE OF BAG

Embroidered Cot Quilt

YOU WILL NEED

- twelve 17 cm (6³/4 in) squares of white homespun
- 50 cm (20 in) of white homespun
- 1 m (1¹/8 yd) of red homespun
- 1 m (1¹/8 yd) of red gingham for the backing
- 1 m (1¹/8 yd) of wadding
- silk embroidery thread, Red
- ordinary sewing thread, Red
- embroidery cotton: Red, White
- usual sewing supplies
- tracing paper
- soft pencil
- 5 cm (2 in) square of heavy cardboard

Note: All the fabrics should be well washed before sewing to ensure they are colourfast.

While this quilt is not strictly appliqué, it does feature charming surface embroidery which makes it fit right in. Take care when choosing the embroidery thread, as it will need to stand up to lots of washing. Certain threads will bleed during washing and may damage your quilt.

Finished size: 62 cm × 92 cm (24¹/2 in × 36¹/4 in)

INSTRUCTIONS

See the patterns on pages 60–64.

1 Using the cardboard as a template, draw sixty squares on the back of the red homespun, leaving a 1 cm (³/8 in) seam allowance around each square. Using the same method, draw forty-eight squares onto the back of the white homespun. Cut out all the squares, leaving a 1 cm (³/8 in) seam allowance around each one.

2 Stitch together twelve Nine-patch blocks, placing the red and white squares as shown in the picture. These blocks should measure 17 cm (6³/4 in) when completed. Put them aside.

Embroidery

1 Using a soft pencil, trace the embroidery shapes onto the centre of the twelve white homespun squares. To make this easier to do, trace the pattern then tape the tracing to a window with the light coming through. Place the homespun square over the top.

2 With the Red silk embroidery thread, stem stitch around each design until all twelve squares are completed.

Assembling

1 Place the squares together with the twelve red and white blocks as shown. Join them in rows of four, then join all the blocks together.

2 Place the gingham fabric right side down, centre the wadding on top, then place the finished top in the middle, right side up. Trim all three pieces to the same size. Baste them together.

3 Cut two strips 5 cm × 60 cm (2 in × 24 in) from the red homespun for the binding. Stitch a strip to the bottom and top edge of the quilt with the right sides together. Cut two more red strips 5 cm × 100 cm (2 in × 40 in) and stitch them to the sides. You may have to adjust these lengths slightly according to your seam allowance. Turn the binding edge over to the back of the quilt, tuck the raw edge under and slipstitch the binding to the back of the quilt, using the Red sewing thread.

4 Using Red embroidery cotton, place a tie in each corner to hold the quilt together, or quilt around each block. I would not recommend using buttons on a small child's quilt.

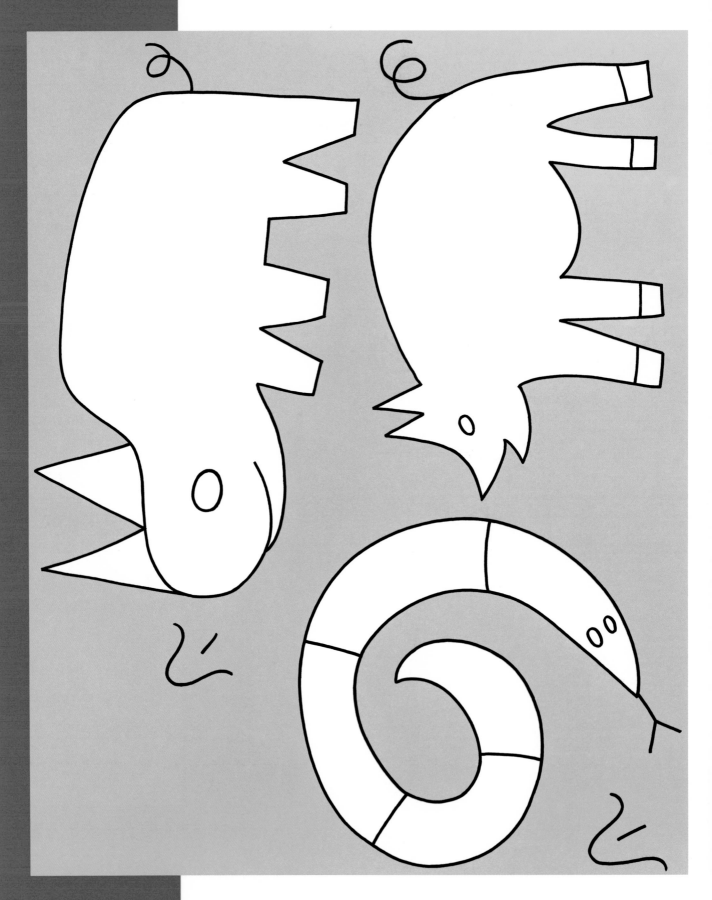

The Love Quilt

This quilt is made up of eighty small blocks. The size of the quilt can be adjusted by adding to or reducing the number of blocks. If you are a beginner, I suggest you start on a smaller version of The Love Quilt.

Finished size: 108 cm × 202 cm (42$\frac{1}{2}$ in × 79$\frac{1}{2}$ in)

INSTRUCTIONS
See the patterns on the Pull Out Pattern Sheet.

Preparation
1 Trace all the appliqué patterns and transfer them to the cardboard. Label and cut them out for templates. Keep all the templates in a large envelope until you need them.
2 Using the picture as a guide, cut out fifty-eight 20 cm (8 in) square blocks in various colours and textures ready for the appliqué. There are eighty blocks in total in this quilt: fifty-eight are appliquéd, seven are pieced and fifteen left plain, using the base fabric as a feature.
3 Cut out the patterns from your selected fabrics, remembering to leave the correct seam allowance for the type of appliqué you are going to do. You can use the traditional paper method of appliqué with a 1 cm (3/8 in) seam allowance or the needleturning method with a 5 mm (1/4 in) seam allowance. For the Vliesofix method, you need not leave any seam allowance at all. Refer to pages 8–9 for the various methods. Appliqué each pattern onto one of the fifty-eight blocks, using the picture as a guide for colour and placement.
4 Embroider the details using the embroidery threads.

Assembling
1 When the fifty-eight appliquéd blocks are completed, lay them out so you can see where the gaps are and fill in with the fifteen plain blocks, taking note of what colours would be best and cutting some of them on the bias for added interest.
2 Fill in the remaining blocks by piecing together any of your favourite quilting designs – for example, Nine-patch blocks, Four-patch blocks, striped blocks and Log Cabin blocks.
3 When all eighty blocks are completed, sew them together in rows of eight blocks across the quilt, then stitch the rows together to complete the quilt top. Try to match the corners of the blocks for a neat look.
4 Cut two 18 cm (7 in) wide border strips and stitch them to the sides of the quilt top. Cut two more border strips the same width and stitch them to the top and bottom.
5 Cut backing fabric to fit the finished size of the quilt top. You will have to make a join in the centre of your fabric.
6 Place the backing fabric, right side down

YOU WILL NEED
- lots of brightly coloured scraps in cotton, velvet, flannel, satin
- 1.5 m (1$\frac{2}{3}$ yd) of fabric for the border
- 1 m (1$\frac{1}{8}$ yd) of fabric for the binding
- 4.25 m (4$\frac{3}{4}$ yd) of fabric for the backing
- queen bed-size wadding
- sixty-three coloured buttons
- embroidery threads, various colours, including Red and Black
- usual sewing supplies
- sewing threads to match the fabrics
- tracing paper
- pencil
- cardboard

with the wadding on top. Place the pieced front on top of the wadding, right side up. Trim all edges to the size of the quilt front. Baste the three layers together.

Quilting

1 Using two strands of Red embroidery thread and a small running stitch, outline quilt around the edge of each block, 1 cm (3/8 in) from the edge. Outline quilt around the appliqué, if you wish. In the same embroidery thread, sew a running stitch around the pieced centre, 1 cm (3/8 in) outside the edge.

2 Tie a button in each corner of the blocks, choosing the colours of the buttons at random. Use six strands of Black embroidery thread for the tying.

TO FINISH

Trim the border edges, then cut four 5 cm (2 in) wide binding strips as long as the edges of the quilt. Sew the two sides first, then the top and bottom. Stitch the binding to the front of the quilt, right sides together, then turn the binding over onto the back. Turn under a small hem and slipstitch the binding in place, using a matching thread.

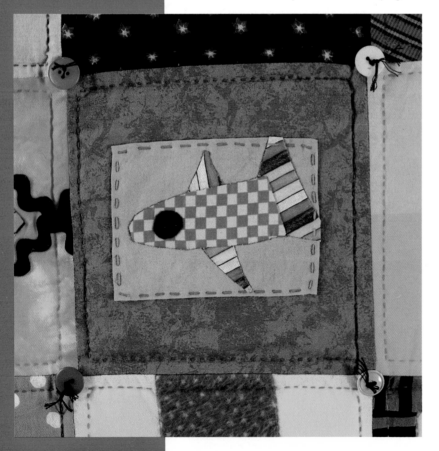

Star Tablecloth

YOU WILL NEED

- **sixteen 35 cm (14 in) squares of cream fabric for the background (the same fabric or a variety of cream fabrics)**
- **1.5 m (1²/3 yd) of cream fabric for the Prairie Point border**
- **1.5 m (1²/3 yd) of yellow cotton fabric**
- **50 cm (20 in) of blue-checked fabric**
- **two pieces of cream homespun, each 70 cm x 136 cm (27¹/2 in x 53¹/2 in) for the backing**
- **stranded embroidery cotton: Yellow, Cream or Beige**
- **sewing threads to match the fabrics**
- **tracing paper**
- **pencil**
- **cardboard**
- **usual sewing supplies**

Stars, stars and more stars are the theme for this summery cloth that would sit proudly on any table. If you find the Prairie Point border a bit daunting, make a simple straight finished edge.

Finished size: 145 cm (57 in) square

INSTRUCTIONS

See the patterns on page 70.

Preparation

1 Trace the star pattern and enlarge it to full size on a photocopier. Transfer it to the cardboard and cut it out for a template. Using this cardboard template, draw sixteen stars on the back of the yellow fabric, taking care to leave enough room for seam allowances between them. Cut out the fabric stars, 1 cm (3/8 in) outside the pencil line.

2 Trace the circle pattern and enlarge it to full size on a photocopier. Transfer it to the cardboard and cut it out for a template. Using this cardboard template, draw 128 circles on the back of the blue-checked fabric, taking care to leave enough room for seam allowances between them. Cut out the circles, 5 mm (¹/4 in) outside the pencil line.

Appliqué

1 Position each star in the middle of a cream square and pin or baste it into place. Appliqué the stars using the needleturn method (see page 8) and the Yellow cotton. Take care to turn under the edge right on the pencil line. Trim the points where necessary, and clip into all the corners. Appliqué stars on all sixteen squares.

2 Using eight of the small circles, gather each one over a cardboard template, using a small running stitch. Press each one well until it is completely flat. Snip the stitching and remove the cardboard.

3 Pin or baste a circle to each point of a star. Stitch them in place, using a small slipstitch and matching thread. Complete all sixteen squares in the same way.

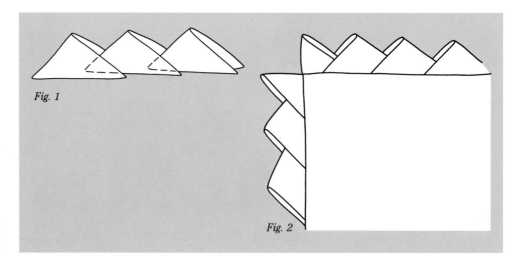

Fig. 1

Fig. 2

Assembling

1 Using a 1 cm (³/8 in) seam allowance, join the squares into four rows of four, then join the rows. Press.

2 For the Prairie Point border, cut twenty-seven 10 cm (4 in) squares from the border fabric for each side. Fold a square in half diagonally, then fold it in half again. Press with a hot iron. Repeat this step for all the squares. To begin assembling the border, slip one triangle into the pocket of the next triangle to the halfway point (Fig. 1). Stitching close to the edge, join twenty-seven border triangles in this way for each side. Pin the border to the right side of the pieced front. Stitch along the same line as before. At the corners, sew halfway along the last triangle, so it can fold back behind itself and halfway along the first triangle of the next side for the same reason (Fig. 2). Gently ease the edge of the tablecloth to fit. Sew the border to the opposite sides of the cloth first, then to the two other sides. Trim any excess fabric and press.

3 Stitch the two pieces of backing fabric together along the long side to form a square. Pin and baste the backing to the pieced front, lining up the centre seams

This pattern is half-size. Enlarge it on a photocopier at 200%.

exactly. Because there is no wadding in this 'quilt', it is very important that these seams are exactly aligned. Trim any excess backing fabric, then turn under a small allowance so the seam of the border is covered. At the corners, fold the last triangle in half towards the back and securely stitch it in place. Repeat for all the corner triangles. Slipstitch the backing into place.

Quilting

Draw a light pencil line 1 cm (³/8 in) inside the outline of each star. Stitch along the pencil line, using two strands of Yellow cotton. Using Cream or Beige cotton, quilt 1 cm (³/8 in) inside each square. Remember, a tablecloth is likely to need regular washing, so the more quilting you do to hold it together, the longer the tablecloth will last.

Red wine and breadsticks, here I come!

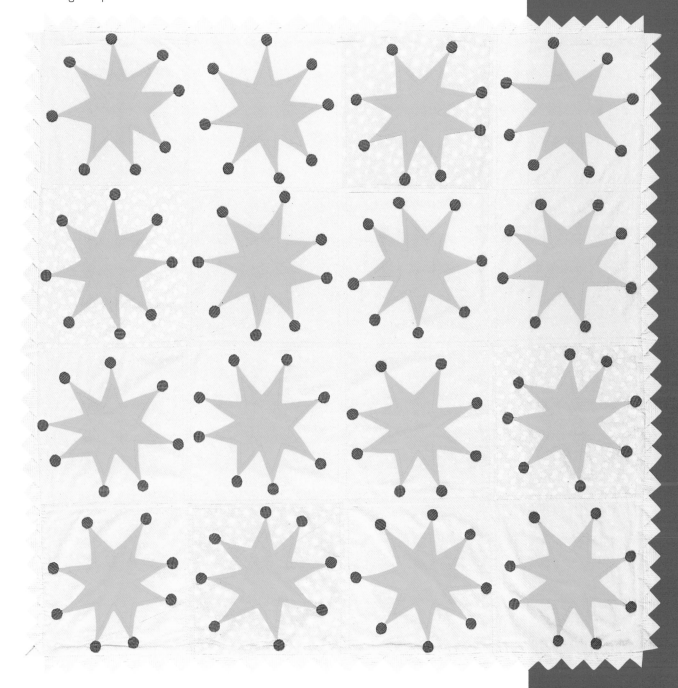

Animal Banner

YOU WILL NEED
- **four 31 cm (12¹/4 in) squares of homespun for the background**
- **scraps of bright plain fabric for the birds and animals**
- **7 cm (2³/4 in) wide scraps for the border**
- **75 cm (29¹/2 in) of fabric for the binding**
- **45 cm x 147 cm (18 in x 58 in) of fabric for the backing**
- **41 cm x 143 cm (16 in x 56¹/4 in) of wadding**
- **embroidery threads in several colours**
- **neutral quilting thread**
- **usual sewing supplies**
- **ordinary sewing threads to match the fabrics**
- **tracing paper**
- **pencil**
- **cardboard**

Note: The appliqué animals can be sewn on using the traditional cardboard method, freezer paper or needleturning.

This banner makes a fun feature in a child's room, hanging over the doorway or over the bed.

Finished size: 41 cm x 143 cm (16 in x 56¹/4 in)

INSTRUCTIONS
See the patterns on pages 74–75.

Appliqué
1. Trace all the parts of the bird and animal patterns and transfer the tracings onto the cardboard. Label each piece carefully. Cut out the shapes and use them for templates.
2. Using the photograph as a guide, trace each pattern piece onto the front of the coloured scraps, leaving room for a 1 cm (³/8 in) seam allowance around each shape. Cut out the shapes with the seam allowances added.
3. Trace the main outline of each animal or bird onto the centre of the background squares. Pin the fabric pieces onto this tracing, using the pencil lines as a guide and referring to the picture for the placement of the pieces. The largest part is appliquéd first, then the smaller pieces are applied on top. The dots can be appliquéd on at the end.

Assembling
1. Cut a selection of 7 cm (2³/4 in) wide fabric scraps into various lengths and join them together at random to make a long strip, approximately 4.5 m (5 yd) long. If the initial strip isn't long enough, you can always add extra pieces at the end.
2. Join the appliquéd squares with a vertical strip between each pair and one at each end. Sew another pieced strip along the

top and bottom of the row.
3. Cut two pieces from the binding fabric, each 4 cm x 45 cm (1¹/2 in x 18 in). Stitch one to each side of the front of the banner, with the right sides together. Cut two lengths 4 cm x 145 cm (1¹/2 in x 57 in). Stitch these to the top and bottom. Press well.
4. Lay the pieced top, right side up, on top of the wadding. Then place both on top of the wrong side of the backing piece. The top piece will be larger than the other two because of the strips which have been added for the binding. Make sure all the pieces are flat and centred, then baste all three layers together ready for quilting.

Quilting
With the neutral quilting thread, stitch around each square, then around each bird or animal and all the detail on them. Using three strands of embroidery thread, stem stitch or back stitch the legs, twigs, tusks and all the other embroidery details, using the pattern as a guide. The birds and animals can be embellished with any amount of embroidery or beadwork – this is entirely up to you. Finally, work the diagonal quilting on the background at an angle of 45 degrees and in rows 4 cm (1¹/2 in) apart. More embroidery can be added on top of the quilting.

TO FINISH
1. Turn the binding (edge of the top piece) over onto the back so only 1 cm (³/8 in) is showing on the front. Trim any excess backing fabric and wadding. Turn under the raw edge and slipstitch the binding in place, using a matching thread.
2. To make each hanging loop, cut and sew

Lamp, cushions and bed throw from the Mosman Storehouse, Mosman NSW

a tube from the binding fabric that is
6 cm × 8 cm (2¹/₂ in × 3¹/₄ in) finished
size. Turn it right side out and press.
Fold it in half and stitch the open ends
together to the back of the banner.
Make one for the top of each vertical
strip. Leave 4 cm (1¹/₂ in) of the loops
showing above the binding.

These patterns are half-size.
Enlarge them on a photocopier at 200%.

These patterns are half-size.
Enlarge them on a photocopier at 200%.

The Spotted Heart

YOU WILL NEED

- scraps of many spotted fabrics
- 26 cm (11 in) square of fabric 1 for the background
- 12 cm x 38 cm (5 in x 15 in) of fabric 2 for the background
- 12 cm x 18 cm (5 in x 7¹/2 in) of fabric 3 for the background
- 12 cm x 10 cm (5 in x 4 in) of fabric 4 for the background
- 8 cm (3¹/4 in) wide strips of spotted fabric for the border
- black fabric for the binding
- 50 cm (20 in) square of thin wadding
- 50 cm (20 in) square of fabric for the backing
- usual sewing supplies
- firm cardboard
- fineline marker pen
- pencil

Long a symbol of love and affection, the heart shape in this little quilt has a special charm. Cut each heart from a different spotted fabric and continue the theme through to the spotted border. The Spotted Heart quilt can also be framed.

Finished size: 50 cm (20 in) square

INSTRUCTIONS
See the pattern on page 79

1 Stitch the centre background square together, following figure1, and placing the fabrics as indicated.

2 Trim the sides to make a 38 cm (15 in) square.

3 With a light pencil line, trace the large heart shape onto the background square. Use this as a guide for appliquéing on the hearts.

4 Make six small heart templates from the cardboard. Pin a cardboard heart

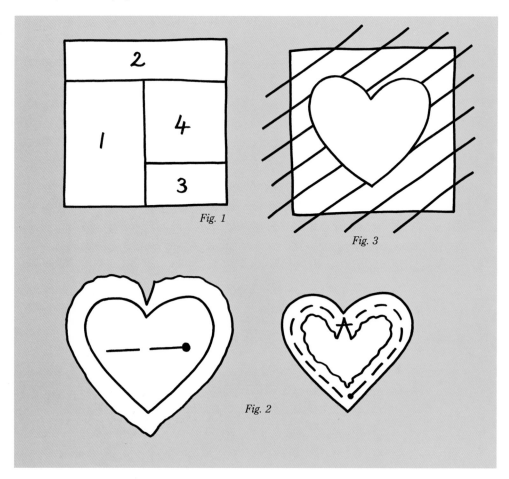

Fig. 1

Fig. 3

Fig. 2

template onto the wrong side of one of the spotted fabrics. Draw round it, using the pencil, then cut it out leaving a 1 cm (3/8 in) seam allowance. Baste the fabric to the cardboard around the edges, cutting in at the V as shown (Fig. 2). Press with a hot iron. Cut the basting thread and carefully take out the cardboard. Cut out and prepare all the hearts in this way. You will need approximately thirty-seven hearts.

Appliqué

1 Place the bottom heart in position on the background square, using the pencil line as a guide. Sew the heart in place with a small slipstitch, using a matching thread. Work with six hearts at a time; stitch them down, then do the next six and so on. Use the photograph as a guide for the placement of hearts and overlap each one as shown.

2 Using the same heart template as before, draw in the centre heart on the background and cut it out. Slip a scrap of spotted fabric under the opening and, using the reverse appliqué method, sew the centre heart (Fig. 3).

For the borders

Sew the spotted fabrics into a long strip, 8 cm (3 1/4 in) wide and having random lengths. Stitch the border to either side of the centre piece, then to the top and bottom. Press the seams to one side.

TO FINISH

1 Place the backing fabric face down, with the wadding on top and the finished top in the centre of the wadding, face upwards. Trim any excess. Baste all three layers together.

2 Cut a 5 cm (2 in) wide binding strip, 2 m (2 1/4 yd) long. Join lengths if necessary. Stitch the binding to the sides, then to the top and bottom. Turn binding to the back and, using a small slipstitch in a matching thread, sew it in place, so that 1 cm (3/8 in) is visible on the front.

3 Make a hanging sleeve on the back.

The pattern for the large heart and appliqué heart are half-size. Enlarge them on a photocopier at 200%.

Acknowledgments

I would like to thank my wonderful husband, Colin, and my understanding family, who have helped make this book possible.
I would also like to thank Karen Fail and Judy Poulos for their support, enthusiasm and patience.